Aviemore Primary School
Milton Park
Aviemore
Invernesshire
PH22 1RR
Tel: 01479 - 810343

This edition first published in 2002 by
Franklin Watts
96 Leonard Street
London
EC2A 4XD

Franklin Watts Australia
56 O'Riordan Street
Alexandria, Sydney
NSW 2015

ISBN 0 7496 4518 0 (pbk)

Dewey Decimal Classification Number 388

A CIP catalogue record for this book is available from the British Library

Printed in Belgium

Editor: Kyla Barber
Designer: Diane Thistlethwaite
Illustrator: Teri Gower

Picture credits: Fiat 12; Hutchison: Nancy Durrell McKenna 14; Honda 10, 11; Image
Bank: 6, 19, Frank Whitney 25; Panos: Jean-Léo Dugast 6-7; QA PHotos Ltd: cover,
18-19; Rex: 24-25; Robert Harding: Kelly Harriger 8-9, Scott Barrow Int'l Stock 13,
Liaison Int 22-23; Zefa: 5, 15, Mathis 16-17, Deuter 20-21, 23, 27.

MACHINES AT WORK

On the Move

Henry Pluckrose

W
FRANKLIN WATTS
LONDON·SYDNEY

People can travel on foot.
But it takes a long time
to get from place to place.

Machines help people
to travel further,
and to carry heavy loads.

A bicycle is a machine.

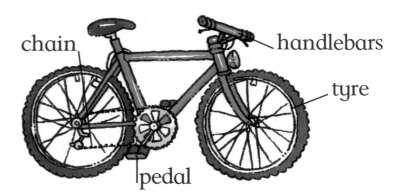

chain   handlebars

tyre

pedal

The faster you pedal,
the faster you move.

You do not need
to pedal a motorbike.

It has an engine that
makes the wheels go round.

Why is this person
wearing a special hat?

11

Cars have four wheels
and the passengers sit inside.
Cars can travel very fast.

But when the roads are busy, a car journey can seem slow and boring.

When a lot of people want
to go to the same place
they can travel together
on a bus or coach.

They can even
travel by tram.

Cars, buses and coaches,
vans and lorries
all use roads.

car fumes

They give off fumes which pollute the air we breathe.

Trains run on specially
built railway tracks.

Some trains travel below ground.

Trains have metal wheels
that fit onto the railway tracks.

Sometimes we need to travel across water.

Hovercraft

Ferry boats have space for lorries, coaches, cars and people.

The ferry doors open to let the vehicles drive on.

FREMONT

Aeroplanes are machines that fly.
A jumbo jet can carry
more than 300 passengers.

The shape of an
aeroplane's wings and tail
helps it to take off.

A helicopter is also a flying machine.

The rocket and
the space shuttle
are also machines.

The space shuttle carries
astronauts into space
and brings them safely
back to earth.

Some people find it
difficult to walk.
What machines
can help them?

Wheelchairs
cannot go up
or down stairs.
They need
special ramps.

bicycle

Hovercraft

Glossary

bicycles have two wheels and two pedals

buses pick up people at bus stops

coaches carry people on long road journeys

ferries carry people, cars and lorries across water

Hovercraft take people and cars across water

motorbikes have two wheels and an engine

trams run on special tracks

space shuttles take astronauts into space

Index

wheelchair

car